FIRST PERSON SORROWFUL

고은

KO UN

FIRST PERSON
SORROWFUL

TRANSLATED BY
BROTHER ANTHONY OF TAIZÉ & LEE SANG-WHA

BLOODAXE BOOKS

ISBN: 978 1 85224 953 3

First published 2012 by
Bloodaxe Books Ltd,
Highgreen,
Tarset,
Northumberland NE48 1RP.

www.bloodaxebooks.com
For further information about Bloodaxe titles
please visit our website or write to
the above address for a catalogue.

Supported using public funding by
**ARTS COUNCIL
ENGLAND**

Cover design: Neil Astley & Pamela Robertson-Pearce.

Printed in Great Britain by
Bell & Bain Limited, Glasgow, Scotland.

ACKNOWLEDGEMENTS

The translators wish to record their deep gratitude to the poet Hillel Schwartz, who with great skill revised the draft translations in the course of several readings, in an attempt to ensure that these versions are both accurate and poetic in English.

Acknowledgements are due to the editors of *Asia Literary Review* and *Modern Poetry in Translation* where some of these translations first appeared. Many thanks are also due to The Poetry Trust for their initiative in bringing Ko Un and his translators to Britain to launch this book at Aldeburgh Poetry Festival and elsewhere, to Andrew Motion for agreeing to write the Foreword, and to LTI Korea.

CONTENTS

FOREWORD

A few years after they met at a poetry reading in Seoul in 1990, Allen Ginsberg wrote a preface to an American edition of translations into English of poems by the Korean poet Ko Un. Ginsberg called him 'a magnificent poet, [a] combination of Buddhist cognoscente, passionate political libertarian, and naturalist historian'. The praise was well deserved. Yet despite this advocacy – and the publication of more than forty translations of his work in Western languages, including twelve in English, Ko Un remains less well-known among poetry lovers in the West, in Britain especially, than he deserves to be. He is a major poet, who has absolutely compelling things to say about the entire history of South Korea, and equally engrossing things to say about his own exceptionally interesting life and sensibility.

The reasons for the ignorance in the West of Ko Un's work – and of Korean poetry generally – are complicated. Some have to do with historical pressures: with the restriction of the Korean language during the Japanese occupation during the first part of the 20th century; with the turbulence during the Korean War (1950-53); and with the period of censorship that followed – on both sides of the border. Some have to do with matters closer to home. With our characteristic indifference to literature in translation, and our suspicions about the re-casting of poetry in particular. And (supposing we manage to overcome that) with our assumption that if Asian literature departs from the aesthetics of Chinese and Japanese poetry (with its powerful emphasis on beauty), it must in some way be second-rate.

These problems are lamentable in various ways and to various degrees. And they're exacerbated by something else – which should in fact be a reason for praising Ko Un. He is an extraordinarily prolific poet: the author of 150 volumes of poetry, fiction and essays – among them *Maninbo* (Ten Thousand Lives), which runs to thirty volumes, and *Paektu-san*, which runs to seven volumes. Of quick and suggestive Zen poems, as delicate as handwriting on water. Of robust gossipy poems. Of joke-poems. Of poems that are squally with anger and compassion. Of love poems. Of political poems.... Taken all in all, it is a truly remarkable range of achievement. But it can seem almost literally dazzling.

All these things make the publication of *First Person Sorrowful* a significant event. It gives an overview of Ko Un's recent work by focusing (with a very few exceptions) on poems he has written in the last ten years. It indicates why we should think of him as a national poet, deeply engaged with national themes, but at the same time as a very personal one. It is exceptionally well-translated. And it allows us to see that despite the great variety of his writing Ko Un is in fact a very concentrated poet.

His abiding concern is nothing less than the quintessentially human question of what it means to live in time. On page after page in this book, in a wonderful cascade of different forms and registers, we find him squaring up to the paradoxes this entails. One minute he is demonstrating a deep apprehension of long geological time ('the gulls lost their ocean. / They cried aloud. / They have continued their lives / through a second generation, a twelfth, even a 1302nd'); the next he is intensely involved with the business of living at a particular moment: 'Today, too, the glow of the setting sun is glorious!'. One minute he is looking back at the past with regret ('In that obtuse period, / all I hoped for was storms that would jolt me breathless'); the next he is criticising the desecrations of the present: 'All of the Korean peninsula is turning into Seoul. / Oh shit, a country with a crush on glitz.'

Given a less steady temperament, and a less accommodating imagination, we might expect our travels through these different time-zones to feel zigzag or even queasy. In fact the prevailing movement of the poems is oddly consoling – because it is circular. Which is to say that Ko Un responds to the almost-infinite variety of things-in-themselves (and of his perceptions) by making every new beginning seem like part of a process of returning, and by transfiguring every 'now' into a link with 'then'. This of course says something interesting about the way in which he sees time itself. It also acts as a framework for the way in which he interprets his own life and the life of others operating within time. Individuals are individuals, and valued for their originality, but their experience cannot avoid being part of a process. In the same way, personal interests cannot help becoming political matters, and national issues inevitably join international ones.

These connections seem especially compelling thanks to the physicality with which Ko Un writes about them. Yet this physicality itself embraces a paradox, for the striking reason that Ko Un generally mixes the allegorical with the elemental. Sure, he enjoys writing about ordinary things. But the recurring motifs of his poems are generic clouds, rivers, flags, winds and skies, and over the course of this book they create a panorama that feels at once very particular and highly abstracted, and a style that is both familiar and original – a kind of amplified Symbolism.

These different kinds of cohesion – principled, spiritual, philosophical, argumentative, stylistic – all converge on the same point. For Ko Un range does not mean diffusion but unity. His hungry appetite for experience, the rapidity with which he synthesises it, the nervous energy of his rhythms: all these things are the hallmarks of a poet whose particular interest is to inhabit each moment as it passes, and yet to see all moments flowing endlessly into one another. This is the process by which he inhabits himself and other people. It is what makes him his own man, and a most eloquent citizen of the world.

ANDREW MOTION

FROM

Poetry Left Behind

(2002)

A Recent Confession

What has become of those white-wept maelstroms
of my sobbing in deepest night?
So much sorrow has slid from my spine.
All expostulations are futile.
The agony that clung doggedly to my shoes, day after day,
that too is gone.
Windswept, the winter port
seems burdened by freight on its way out
and by freight just off-loaded,
but my heart today is void, nothing within.

In the Nangok hilltop slum
the gaunt children of those breathlessly narrow alleys
survive with vacant eyes;
on the TV screen at newstime
Afghan children barely survive breathing dust
on hills without a blade of grass,
but I, I am not hungry.

Gone too my helplessly naïve days of drunkenness,
days when I thought to butter up chumps buying me drinks
only at last to curse them out.

During those thirty bygone years,
all the mud-flat tossing and turning under dictatorship
gave rise in us (such paradox!) to hope,
to a passion for existence.

Now, having turned my arse on the sea,
I can't hold on to a single phrase of Rachmaninov
and his rib-grinding strings.
Once past the graves of those bygone years,
what glory can there be in my soul's proletarian wilderness?
I am merely a tall spirit-post standing in the wind.

Song of the Forest

It was November.
I parted from my retreating friend.
Turning my back on his hacking cough,
I left fictions behind and entered the forest,
which knows no defilement.
As if prolonged anticipations had piled up,
though no one around was anxiously waiting,
the forest throbbed on all sides,
embracing even the waving dreams of fresh leaves
that would bud months later.
I was alive, pulse beating, lucky –
an empty forest all to myself.

I love the countless, lingering regrets.
After glancing back more than once
toward the village where my friend had gone,
I went farther into the already darkening forest.
Oblivious of glory,
the road did not know whose road it was.

What should I fear now?
At the appearance of one unexpected unassuming visitor,
the naked branches opened their eyes in the dark
and the wind in the forest rose. To my puzzlement:
for that was when unceasing winds had died down in the world outside.

I was born in a land with far more adjectives than nouns.
I longed to be in touch with wordless earth,
covered with the dead leaves of all the trees
that had, each one, fallen in sorrow
before ever being stuck with a name.
At every step my soles felt dazzled
as if little flowers were blooming beneath them.

The Bronze Age is past.
One last breath of wind remained,
and I could not see now the infinite trembling of empty treetops
with their premonitions of other winds that must follow.
I had made too fine a point of bitterness
and ecstasy.
Wherever I went, errors abounded.
Here I quietly let go of my greed
for right answers.

The forest was a sanctuary of pure hearts.
I heard the fluttering wings of birds returning late.
Having given away everything,
the forest itself was empty
of all but its memory as a place
where generations of animals were reborn as other animals.

I hesitated... should I go farther in?
Perhaps night desired a respite of truth
after midday's lies of themselves withdrew.
I heard a hitherto unheard song coming from... somewhere.
Surely the one singing wasn't that friend from whom I'd parted,
so who else could it be
but me?
I could not tell.
I could not tell.
My whole body was awake, listening
to what might be my song in the next life.

I whispered a warning to myself:
Don't go on.
Don't go any farther.

Eventually I convinced myself to go on, saying:
Love fiction, there is a blessing in it.
Go farther.

After the Plaza

A light drizzle is falling now.
The ideology of the Plaza is over and done with.
The crowd of more than a million who gathered that year
went back home
one by one.
They have long since dispersed.
Each one went back home
to a solitary cocoon.

They crept into their beloved cyber world.

One evening
somebody came rushing out shouting:

Oh, there has to be dictatorship.
There has to be a coup d'état.
Only then
will the white bones in our tombs
come rushing out with irreproachable wrath.
Abandoning their twelve daily snoozes,
they will rush from their cocoons.
Only then will the Plaza be filled with creatures of a rising tide.

A light drizzle is falling now.
No one is flying into a rage..
Drizzle is falling and cars are stuck in traffic.
But remember, old friends,
this Plaza was where we began, always.

The Small Mountains of Asia

Asia's century of humiliation was its due.
Now spit it all out.
The Yi Ching's eight hexagrams,
old phlegm, spit them out,
out into yon puddle.
After that,
give modernity the heave-ho.

Look back.

Who does not know the great Himalayas?
The Kunlun Mountains,
the Altai Mountains, who does not know them?
Those splendid names
are not simply the names of mountains
but of something overwhelming –
of splendour,
greatness,
sublimity.

But today, turning my back on their highnesses,
I want to bow to the little mountains everywhere across Asia.
In the Himalayas, they rarely give names to mountains
less than eight thousand metres high.
But today, after sunset,
I want to bow to mountains
less than a thousand metres high,
to a throng of those mountains,
calling each by its venerable name.

Just about forever, throughout Asia,
mountains have stretched before us.

They hold my wishes
and my children's future;
on their slopes they hold the splendid fresh green of May.

In Asia, mountains also rise up
behind villages.
There, villagers find their ancestors' graves.
There, bare beech branches shake nightlong.
In Asia's subtropics
and tropics, they find
long-haired, drooping shadows all around.

I want to grow old visiting
the nameless little mountains in every corner of Asia,
those that have no splendour,
no greatness,
no sublimity.
I want to die calling out their names one by one.
I want to bow one last time with all my pint-size remorse
on the side of a small mountain
under the indigo sky of dawn.

Little mountains,
little mountains, Suni Mountains, Jeong-Hwa Mountains,
homes of Asia's true philosophies, Chilsung, Samnyong.

Suni, Jeong-Hwa, Chilsung, and Samnyong are all common, unassuming
Korean names. [Tr.]

Memoirs

I was twenty.
World-weary for no reason,
I loathed the springtime when apricots bloomed.
I starved.
I wanted to fall
Bang!
on the bitterly cold snowfields
of Irkutzk in Siberia, forty below zero.
I wanted to fall, shot dead, like a young Decembrist.

In that obtuse period,
all I hoped for was storms that would jolt me breathless.

A shaking wrist was slashed by a straw-cutter.
When a hoe was thrust into the earth's flesh,
the earth went wild with weeping.

I was sixty.
I dismissed every kind of triviality.
Above all, I disdained belated excuses.
As ever,
I was revolted by lovely clear days,
had to run out,
rapt with joy,
to the far side,
to the far side of the plains
whose flesh through dark clouds was being struck
by knife-blades of thunder and lightning.

Away with every kind of resignation.
Away with every kind of nirvana.

Even after sixty, I have been inescapably, helplessly childish.
All I have are a few friends,
and one lung.
I had to head in the other direction
on account of the lung I had lost.
Still I bear in mind Che Guevara, that evening star, my belated
      discovery.

The latter half is an explosion of the first half.

Autumn Song

Who will hold funerals for falling leaves?
There should be paradoxes.
We have no need of family,
of nation.
The leaves that fall
rustling, blown by the wind,
wish for nothing.

God is ultimately meaningless.
That's why he exists.

Sobering up after drink,
I went to where applause was ringing
then turned round sharply.

Who is he?

Vanity grew wild
even in dreams,
so he himself was immured by it.
Everything was desolate, even in dreams.

Who is he?

There were only two roads.

Quietly, he turned toward the designated place,
braving the thorns.
Unskilled arrows came flying.
They said:
He's coming, he's coming.

Surrounded by countless pointing fingers,
denied even a syllable of explanation,
harrassed by the jaundiced power of archaic institutions,
he reached a village shack.
Here and there some pain
remained after drawing out the arrows.
Fields after harvest lay empty, sleepless,
but in the forest beyond, leaves destined to fall
were still awaiting the wind.

Solitude is shining through.
Who is he?
He is autumn.
He is a dead friend.

That Path in the Forest

On that path through the forest remain traces of tribes,
so it stays snug a long while.
Those coming after are never strangers, never enemies.

Despite the strong wind blowing outside,
the forest within
was almost windless.
It was like the whispering
of a sacred book,
and as virtuous as my deceased wife.

I went farther in.
Fallen fruits, clustered together, were fermenting slowly.
Ah, the smell of wine!

Was that Odin?
A dappled deer, surprised, vanished just over there.
I looked around
hesitantly
as if my mother, who left the world young
and in my childhood
had just returned.
There was an ancient yearning in my surprise.
I too must be surprised a few times more in my life.

I have to go back to the Age of Friends from the Age of Tribes.
That's why every path in the forest leads to the world outside.

Arriving at a brief moment between absence and existence,
I came across a solitary spring in the depths of the forest.
The water had long been praying.

I have to go on to the Age of Friends, away from the Age of Tribes.
That's why every path in the forest leads to the world beyond.

Time with Dead Poets

We are in one sector of the universe, sometimes a wilderness,
sometimes a womb.
Now each of us
is not just an individual living poet.
Here
we are also unfamiliar backcountries
made up of something different
from living poets.

No sound passes beyond the boundaries of extinction.
Our bodies sometimes feel heavy,
sometimes lighter than our hearts.
The souls of dead poets
enter and make their abode in each of our bodies,
folding their weary wings.
I am more than myself.
You are more than yourself.
We sing in the universe's dialect,
sing in the new mother-tongue of dead poets.
We begin alone,
then we are together all the time.

When huge waves rose suddenly
only to settle back the next morning,
when the gulls emerged from hiding
after the terror,
no longer a-tremble,
and went soaring high, drawing the most refined circles,
a person died.
A poet, people whispered.

At times, a day is as long as a slowly writhing intestine;
at times, a day is as short as a newborn gull's wings.
It's because the dead poet's remaining lifetime has settled
inside each of our lives born of the egg-laying myth.

In the void above high plateaux at 5000 metres
a dry, gaunt Tibetan gull is flying.
A very, very long time ago,
a continent came rushing near, collided.
Then what had been a sparkling sea
went mad and turned into the Himalayas.
The gulls lost their ocean.
They cried aloud.
They have continued their lives
through a second generation, a twelfth, even a 1302nd...
Each succeeded the next.
And the next.
Their cries at last became songs, became poems.

So each of us
is a living poet.
We are each not only a living poet;
we need to be three poets, seven poets, eleven, in this world and
        the world after.
We are the very sensuality
of the time in which we come and go.
When we hold a memorial for someone,
that is also the time when someone will hold a memorial for each
        of us.
Our meeting here
is our leaving many partings behind
in many other places, elsewhere.

Here we are!

In our backcountry there is a lake.

On the water's surface, before and after we close our eyes,

floats a white water lily.

Unfortunate is the poet who has never written an elegy for someone.

On that account we must sometimes write a new elegy.

That is another name for a love song. A flower.

Ah! we so need sorrow.

The lake remembers the middle of its ancient sea.

A Boy's Song

The reason why that sea without ancestors
breaks in waves like that, day after day,
is because it longs to become the sky.
It cannot be otherwise!

The reason why that sky
foolishly, day and night,
produces clouds
and then erases them
is because it longs to come down to the sea.
It cannot be otherwise!

The reason why I cannot live on my own like an empty bottle,
why I cannot live only with kith and kin,

is because I long to become someone else, if just once...
Otherwise,
I'll have to live in ignorance of the countless others
surrounding me in this world.

You people!
Marvel at the boy. Marvel at the boy's song.

Places I Want to Go

Thirty years ago
I had places I wanted to go.
I was everywhere on a map
of a scale of 1,000,000: one.
Twenty years ago
I had places I really wanted to go.
The blue sky that kept returning to me through the bars of my
        cell window
was my road.

Thus far I have managed to plod here and there.

But I have set a few places aside.
After I have quit this world
the places I want to go
will keep on waiting for someone to come.

I had places I wanted to go.
When flowers fell,
when flowers fell in the evening,
I straightened up,
closed my eyes.

My Next Life

I entered the forests of Mount Seo-un. Home at last!
I breathed a long sigh.
Shadows lay heaped on shadows.
I let go the few drunken rays of light
I had brought with me. Night fell.

In every country without fail freedom was at an end.

I also let go, bit by bit,
the past hundred years' garbage.
The next morning
drops of dew were hanging in empty cobwebs.

There were too many pasts in the world. The future had shrunk.
Elements of the wind beyond
nuzzled into the forest.
The oak leaves were twittering like returning birds.
Looking back,
I knew I came from generations of illiterates.

Somehow,
Somehow,
I have been caught in the inescapable letters of an agglutinating
        language.

In my next life I will be a breathless stone
deep beneath the ground,
under a mute widow's skeleton
and the new, silent corpses of several orphans
bundled in straw sacks.

Spring Days Are Passing

Surrender everything like this:
flowers are falling.

Let it all go like this:
the evening tide holds nobody back.

Layers in the sea:
jellyfish,
filefish,
sea squirts,
rockfish,
flatfish, sea bass,
barracuda,
plaice like grandmother's fan,
and right at the bottom: sea anemones.
Needless to say
life continues after certain death.

There should be more sins on earth.
Spring days are passing.

White Mountains

In October 1999, three of us went to the White Mountains in New Hampshire. Somewhere near the house where Robert Frost once lived, lagging behind, I lost my way. Completely surrounded by deep scarlet leaves, I found myself condemned to solitary confinement for life. Buried in waves of autumn leaves, I could not help but collapse wildly. Helplessly, I began to call the names of places I had left behind. As if drunken, randomly, as if drunken, with no order:

Noryangjin
Geum River
Mapo
Yalu River
Unmun temple on Cheong-do Island
Hamheung
Mokpo
Nakdong River
Daejeon
Pohang
Julpo in Buan
Wangsimni
Daedong River
Geomun-do Island
Seorak-san
Nine-Dragon-Pool in the Outer Diamond Mountains
Seoguipo
Cheonji
Soyang River
Nam River in Jinju
Mungyeong
Soyang River
Naksan-sa temple by the East Sea
Mallipo

Songak-san in Gaeseong
Mangyeong River
Nangnim-san
Gurye
Gogun-san in Dongnae
Hye-san Samsu Gap-san...

I came to my senses.
I was no lifer, no first offender.

I simply told myself:
every place in this world is guiltless
and I have somewhere to go back to
with $160 in my pocket.

Another day
in another place, too,
there is sure to be somewhere to go back to
with no original sin.

Already wasteful lights were shining in the second parking lot.

The places named are all in Korea. [Tr.]

Poetry Left Behind

If it's possible, if it's really possible,
why should there not be times when we start over again
from our mother's womb
as if a newborn.
Life always has to listen alone
to the sound of the next wave.

Still, we should not turn back from the road once taken.
Tatters of the years while I wandered about
are flapping here and there
like laundry.

When I was poor even tears were lacking.

Some nights
I warmed my cold back at a dwindling bonfire,
then, turning cheerlessly, warmed my breast.
Some other nights
I simply froze, and shuddered, trembling.

Whenever countless tomorrows became today
I was often a stranger in a back seat.
At dusk the mountains were so deep
that the road I had to take
seemed longer than that which I had taken.

The wind blew...
It blew...

Was that a spirit howling once, or poetry?

Sorrow is never something we sell or buy.
So, be sorrowful
as a lamp
standing far beyond.

There should be nothing that I have left,
but feeling there was something
I had left behind
as fog was lifting,
I rose quickly from the spot where I had been staying,
likely on the west coast
near the outermost tip of Tae-an Peninsula.

Was that a soul howling at some period of my life, or poetry?

Armistice Line

Today again the sun is setting.
The tight-lipped ridges
and valleys are
opening wide their heart-hollows,
and the sun is setting along the 155 miles of the Armistice Line.

How I long to shout
like a mute, like a...
What words could remain
at the ice-crusted headwaters of the Imjin River?
What could remain
in those Baekma Highlands, in Daesung Mountain,
in the rusted helmets below Hyangno Peak?

Fifty years of Armistice Line have passed in a flash
at the constricted waist of our land.
They have passed on wings beating quicker than agonised love.
There were days of snowstorm.
At high noons of hatred,
not minding who went first
they should have laid down their stand-off guns,
should have buried them
in the thick snow-flurries,
should have buried them all
in the day-long songs of cuckoos.

All those years every word was a lie.
All those years the roaming souls of the fallen
alone have spoken the truth.

Fifty years of division have passed.

Today again the sun is setting on 155 miles of barbed wire.
For what do I sing now, coughing blood,
if some day I should visit here again?
Don't blame me for singing.
Today again the sun is setting in silence.
Darkness comes without our waiting.

Io Island

I will go to Io Island.
Across the sea, beyond horizons
the colour of dry pumpkin,
leaving my despair behind, I will go to Io Island.
Oh, my country! Let me leave.
I will leave behind desolate hours and fields,
and the womb from which I came.
I will even abandon my beloved old house.

Legs wounded, skin peeling,
I will row to the sea
with oars of bare bones.
Like a baby fish, I have been thrown into despair.
The sea is a place where descending seagulls find rest.

I will go to Io Island.
The land expands by itself.
The sea, too, expands by itself until it reaches Io Island.
Oh, my country! Let me leave.
Leaving women, a few possessions and the grave
in another's ground where I should be secretly buried
I will go to Io Island. I will abandon the place where I have lived so long.

I will go to Io Island, leaving my despair behind.
Across the sea,
the sun will set on the trembling horizon.

Then a new light will rise above Io Island,
from the long-cursed night, and day will break.
Leaving behind my deepest despairs, I will go
to Io Island, toward the dazzling light.

This poem, written in the mid-1960s when the poet in his early 30s was sojourn-
ing in Jeju Island, disappeared and was unexpectedly recovered in 2000. [Tr.]

24 little songs

*

At the edge of a reed field
mallard ducks, about to leave,
are pluming their feathers
for yet a little while.

*

Morning has arrived so solemnly!
With no place for me, I go back inside.

Leaves, still green on the hill, fade to your hearts' content.

*

A chrysanthemum white with frost: that was her beginning.
A peony wet with dew: that was her end.

Today and once again,
she is the flower's beginning and end

*

A comet disappeared.
In the light of the sun
beyond the Earth
the comet shone, then, shining, disappeared.

*

A cold wind
stirs
the yellow feathers of the baby chicks.

Chicks' legs stay thin for a long time.

*

Imje shouts,
Duksan hits with a stick.
Meanwhile
the hill in front of us turns the other way round and becomes
        the hill behind.

Confound you!
You rascal!

Imje & Duksan were Seon (Zen) Masters of the Tang Dynasty. These lines
are emblematic of their different approaches in guiding disciples toward en-
lightenment, which might sometimes arrive at a single stroke. [Tr.]

*

A thump!
like the sound of a huge rock being dropped.

Was it a sound made by the darkening mountain?
After,
the owl's eyes became bigger.

*

Maybe the next life exists because of remorse?
Shabby mule,
next time, I'll be a mule and
you a human being I won't be sorry to carry a long way.

*

In the stable where to the bitter end a sick horse refused to kneel down
a faint light of dawn is spreading.
It was a long night,
a long long night.

*

Grandfather spoke slowly:
You have a long way to go.
Don't hurry,
go plodding along like an ox
and rest every so often.

*

The falling leaves dance as they fall.
When I quit this world
I too will dance as I go.

*

Do I have the love of one person
that can wash away the hatred of several people?
I had been opening an umbrella,
but I closed it again,
and just welcomed the rain.

*

I asked a child:
Do you want to be a beggar,
or a thief?

The child asked:
Why, is there nothing
but that in this world?

Indeed so. In this world, there is only the Caspian Sea and the
     Black Sea.

*

I am caught in spring snow.
Catching a cold
like love,
my skinny body is caught in spring snow.

*

Let go
of the things you have spent thirty years shouting for.

Among them,
justice!
Let go of it forever.

*

One day in March I looked down at the Mongolian desert.
It looked like my father.
It looked like the face of my mother.

Above all, I felt ashamed of myself.

*

On top of a heap of garbage by the roadside
a trashed electric fan
is turning eagerly in the cold wind.

Passing by, I stopped there for a long time.

*

Ten years, thirty years, or fifty years,
if such time-spans were not transient,
if such life-spans were not transient,
humans would have become much more barbarous.

Oh, long live sublime transience!

*

Today
may be a trivial day,
the day someone is being born,
someone is leaving,
someone waiting.

Today too, the glow of the setting sun is glorious!

*

As if saying, 'Forget, forget!'
the crescent moon is passing into a cloud.

*

Scarlet rhododendrons are in blossom.
The crape myrtle trees beyond have no thought of blossoming.

So everything in the world has its own way of living. Glad of that,
    I wander on.

*

Lee Moon-Jae told me what he saw
while he was covering the Diamond Mountains Marathon.

He said he saw the snow
falling in a very orderly fashion
then piling up
without the slightest scattering,
as if being shaken out of a sieve,
as if being martyred.

47

He also realised that
snow is really white,
very white,
its flakes making each other shine.

Wonderful!

*

With the least reason
one would laugh easily,
one would burst into tears.
They have all
been buried, laughter and tears left behind.

Graves covered with snow.

*

Zen koans are a trap, a pit.
A tiger falls into a pit and can't get out again. Silly koan!

FROM

Late Songs

(2002)

Ruins

When I was just twenty,
everywhere I went was in ruins.

During the nights of curfew,
wide awake, I often inclined more to death than to life.

Ruins didn't easily change
into something.
They didn't change into something,
and weren't born to cry as other babies.

The war did not end in my heart.

Fifty years later
I saw the ruins in this city.
I was still a piece of broken brick in the ruins
in this ostentatious city.

The oil-lamp lights of those days are gone now,
but the post-ruin age has not reached me.

Song of White

One life
dreams of another life.
Late spring white pear blossoms, their hearts throbbing,
await the moon.

One life
resembles another life.
In the summer night, the field of buckwheat flowers
awaits the moon.

One life
inhumes another life.
It's winter.
The snow that fell heavily yesterday
awaits the moon with all its heart.

I throw a stone.
Buried in the snow,
it begins another life.

Finally the moon rises.

I

I was all things in Nature.
I was a ladybird,
a cow,
a red ant,
a yaksa demon,
an oak tree,
and a bug on an oak tree.
I was a beetle,
then, having died,
left my beetle shell in a spider's web swaying in the wind, and set off.
I was a salmon that never returned,
a pond snail,
a poisonous snake in July. The snake's skin was sacred.

I wanted to become a dog
but was the descendant of the most barbarous clansmen in the world.
I was a pedlar
devoured by a tiger.
I was a maggot,
and will be a maggot again.

I
was a hare,
and as a hare
was caught and devoured by a wild boar,
then was born as one of a boar's litter. I disliked wisdom.

Born as a human being
I was an awkward shaman,
then my human shape was cast off.
I was an egg broken
before it became a chick,
a goose worn-out from flying day and night, seven thousand kilometres.

I was an oddjobber in a crossroad tavern in Cheonan late in the
        Goryeo Dynasty,
and a boatman at Buan
in the mid-Yi Dynasty.

I shall be an amoeba. I shall howl and howl on moonlit nights.

Goryeo Dynasty, 936-1395 AD; Yi Dynasty, 1396-1910 AD. [Tr.]

A Blizzard

I was in a blizzard.
Home was far off,
there were so many things in the world I did not know.

What teacher could be there for me?
I met up with myself alone,
cried alone,
stopped crying alone.

What friend could be there for me?
I lost the way alone.
Alone I walked on and on.

I was in a blizzard.
I was a mountain animal
that climbed down into the village.
In my childhood
I cried in a blizzard all day long,
and yesterday I was an animal that did not cry.

One Day

Several elephants are following their daily route.
Near Lumbini, in Nepal,
this being the dry season,
the forest is extremely sparse.
As they advance
they come across a dead elephant.

Together they carry the corpse
with their trunks,
bury it in an uninhabited spot
away from watching eyes.

Moving on,
they come across the bones of another dead elephant.
These they clear away with their feet, kicking.

An aged elephant among them
sends a call to its mate on the slopes of the Himalayas
saying it can walk no farther.
From far off comes the response:
Very well.
Let's meet again in the next life.

The elephant stealthily drops behind,
heads for a place unknown to anyone.
It leaves the world in such a way
that no one can tell
if it is alive or dead.

The elephant knows its past life and next life.
A cloud descends
into a puddle.
That day a human child is born at the roadside,
to be called Siddhartha, or whatever.

A Poem

One day
it was a guest.

One day
it was the host.

All those years
each of the chimneys was dreaming
of the smoke it would send up.

Today I'm still not sure who a poem is.

First Person Sorrowful

I am sad. Enlightenment soon becomes a contradiction.
After the revolution early last century
the Soviet poets
decided they would only say 'We'.
They decided they would only call themselves
'We'.
They were enchanted.
Their decision held
even when they could not go out into the streets,
even when they lingered indoors
due to heavy blizzards.
They took oaths saying 'We...'
by themselves.
'I' had disappeared somewhere
deep in the looking-glass.
Mayakovsky, too, one bright sunny day, dashed out
shouting and shouting 'We'.
He was a poet of the street.
'I' was not allowed anywhere.
'I' was wicked.
'We'
'We...'
That alone had incantatory power.

Little by little, a low-pressure front settled in.
Summer flowers kept being trampled.
Revolution
devoured revolution.
The air went out of every child's ball.
Likewise the taut round atmosphere
of 'We'
slowly went flat.

Someone boldly wrote
'I am in love',
but still, as long the custom,
it was read, 'We are in love'.
Winter snows had not all melted.
Spring is always uncertain.

Late last century
the Soviet Union disappeared.
Countries dropped out of the Warsaw Pact
one after another.

Since then
poets have nothing but 'I'.
Starting with 'I'
they end the day with 'I'.
There is nothing
except 'I'.
God, too, is another name for 'I'.

Today I bury
the ghosts of 'We' and 'I' in the endless waves of the Pacific Rim.
Who will be born?
Who will be born,
neither 'We' nor 'I'?
Each wave is one wave's grave, another wave's womb.

An earlier version of this poem was included in *Songs for Tomorrow*. [Tr.]

To a Tree

You were shaken
by a storm
for three whole days,

shaken
to the roots.

Yet today
you are standing motionless, your whole body in stillness,
unaware of a breath of wind.

Ah, you are standing motionless
ahead of days when you will be shaken again and again,
tens or hundreds of thousands of times.

The world spurns lies.

It's

It's a heart throbbing,
tears dripping from the muzzle of a gun.

It's
subtracting rather than adding up,
dividing rather than multiplying.

It's
listening.

It's
a bowl of rice.

It's
underground roots
not having to worry about the leaves up above.

It's
someone's childish fluting.

It's every kind of life,
each individual life
not subject to other lives.

It's
the sight of harnessed oxen plowing fields in days gone by.
Alas!
oxen's millennial yokes.

It's
a father dying ahead of his son.

It's
a mother tongue.

It's
one person's blood warming another person's blood.

It's
a mother for whom her baby's crying is all.

It's
an archipelago.

It's a person being a human for another human being,
a person being nature for Nature.

It's
myself being finally abolished

Ah, Peace!

An earlier version of this poem was included in *Songs for Tomorrow*. [Tr.]

Full of Shame

(2006)

Has a Poem Come to You?

I opened my breast. The lungs emerged.
Then, at last, the scalding heart.
That hidden future of a thousand years ago
and that all-too-hidden past of a thousand years later,
both now have come forward to shape that mass
we call, today, a face.

Keynote speeches, poor debates.

Is 2000 part of the 20th century or the 21st?
Early in the summer of 2000
in the restaurant of a hotel
beside the artificial lake in Gyeongju
I was studying the water between the cherry trees.
The water was bordered
by too much falsehood.

To combat American imperialism from now on
we should unite,
Pierre Bourdieu told me.
He was three years older than me,
but very boyish.
so accordingly, I too became a boy.

The water was pretending to be unaware
of the lives and deaths held within it.

Today's face
emerges from two masses
lumped together,
France's then,
Korea's now.

Ah, the absoluteness of chance!
Just then
outside the window
one great-tit went flying off.
(A great-tit, I think, and not a sparrow)
My attention,
leaving behind the heat of imperialism,
was fully caught up in that bird,
by the movement of that bird.

Bourdieu asked,
has a poem come to you?
(A bird just lifted off; surely a poem has come to you.)

Only then emerging
from beneath the expanse of water outside the window
I gasped, letting out the breath I'd been holding so long.
I replied as would a blind man soaked through:
Yes, a poem has come.

Together we laughed aloud.
When we laughed
the one had so many wrinkles on his face and neck
that the other's eyes disappeared completely.

Shortly after, Bourdieu crossed over to Japan,
gave a special lecture sponsored by the Fujiwara Publishers,
        went back to Paris.
Soon, he passed away.
I leafed through the 14 volumes
of the Bourdieu Library in the Fujiwara edition.
Then
I read Derrida's and Said's memorial addresses.

Quietly, another poem came.

A Plastic Bag

A black plastic bag
in which I had carried two bunches of chives,

now empty

suddenly borne aloft by a gust of wind

danced alone.

Dancing, it vanished beyond the fence.

Mother!

Ear

From the world
beyond
someone is coming.

Sound of rain at night.

Someone is going there. The two will be sure to meet.

Breath

How peaceful, the face of one who has just breathed his last.
The trail of the breath still remaining
on the slopes of that face
is peaceful.

No mourning, by request.

An Egg-laying Story

In an early-morning dream I saw an ostrich.
Or rather,
before the ostrich,
I saw an ostrich egg.
It was a yellowish, whitish, silent egg.
Before it hatched
some kind of sound came from that egg.
At the sound,
the mother ostrich outside
lowered her head
and murmured.
They were already talking to one another.

In some book
I read that the numinous Kalavinka bird
utters numinous words
while it is still in the egg.

Whether it be ostrich and ostrich egg
or stork and stork egg,
each comes to life in this world from the egg,
so they must have a lot to say to each other.

North Korea

Until when
until when
will you
be my present tense?

Tonight again I shake violently from the aftershocks of a century
of quakes.

Pride

Today there is no temple, no ancestral shrine for me.

I believe in nothing.
With all my bones
I resist the neon signs in the night streets.

Ancestors' arrowheads are still quivering.

Snowfall

A thousand years before, I was you,
a thousand years after, you will be me.

Together, we are listening, all ears.

Late in the night snow is falling.

Soundlessly.
Soundlessly.

We are both listening.

White Butterfly

Behold.
One white butterfly,
ghost of wisdom, is flying
over the foolish sea.

All the books of this world are shut.

My Will

How the river's sorrow is flowing away in the twilight!

The age of the Mahabharata will be gone,
the age of the Book of Odes,
the age of the Chu Ci will come on a moonlit night that's like
       summoned spirits.

The age of Homer will be gone,
the age of Herodotus will come.

The age of heroes will be gone,
you, bird, singing day after day, will have your time.

The time will ripen when humans are human to humans.

How enchanted I will be with my friends' dialects.
After ten thousand years or so,
or more,
when I have been utterly, utterly abolished
will a time come when all wars die?
Ah, let my eyes peer from the skulls on that day!

Mahabharata: ancient Indian war epic.
Book of Odes: songs of everyday life on the riverside of the Yellow River writ-
ten in ancient China.
Chu Ci: shaman songs from around the Yangtze in ancient China. [Tr.]

The Monk Hyecho

When I follow the footsteps of the esoteric teenage monk Hyecho,
my mind cannot help becoming quite blank.
Of a sudden leaving behind the quarrels of his homeland
he went to India by boat,
then walked on dusty roads
through its five nations.

After the harsh five Indias
he entered his thirties breathless on the mountain passes of Kashmir.

He greeted autumn
in the forlorn Taklamakan Desert
where a watermelon seed was sprouting before his foot,
from a seed that had just happened to drop there.
He didn't burst into tears.
Nobody's future life was there.

He never returned
from that hollow desert
around which whirlwinds soar.

Hyecho (704-787 AD) was born in Korea and became a Buddhist Tantric monk
of the Silla Dynasty. He made a journey to India to seek Truth when he was
only in his teens and disappeared without trace. In the 20th century the record
of his pilgrimage was discovered among the books in the library in Dunhuang,
so the story of his life in India and China became known. [Tr.]

October 19

Autumn reveals my bones.
My heart has been
bruised to the core,
it has become the blue sky.

There is no broken-knife lightning,
no thunder.

Yellow Sea at sunset.

No peacock's tail floats on the sea;
on the mountain slopes
and inside their shadows the fallen leaves are blowing about.

The soul regrets.

At the seaside a few shells are playing.
Now I
want to learn nothing.
Oh, my ignorance in the autumn!
I am most grateful to have grown up only in this little country
            south of the Armistice Line.

Look.
Now
there is no soaring chimney smoke in the village at dusk,
no sound of parents calling children.
I would say that this is how we are today.

Autumn Reply

Autumn's come.
The short postman left grumbling
after delivering a letter that'd gone somewhere else first.
Outside the gate,
very ancient things
are being reborn as new things still unnamed.
It's the same even on the roundabout path hardened with pebbles.
In the sky,
every doubt's vanished.
Beneath the sky
the life remaining in the autumn leaves
is fresh beneath my eyebrows.
Young rice plants that sprouted from the stubble after harvest,
they're also fresh.

The shadows of the maple trees have doubled in length.
My spirit, however, drags.
How can I greet this autumn
with nothing but agonies
and a thousand varieties of vanity?

Only when the soul's light
can it enter the other world, ten thousand billion lands away.
Now, in this world,
autumn's come.
How fortunate.

It's not always been so fortunate.
Autumn's come, yes.
There's nothing to regret.
A wind's blowing
that would be lighter
than ash from a fire.

The hairs on my head
rise lightly.

One breath of wind
speaks, turning over the fallen leaves.
What are you are talking about?
Is it love? Or the vanity of love?

I am ashamed.

Love doesn't belong to today, it's always something gone by.
The burning briquette stove
all night long absorbs that hot love.
I dare not open my eyes
and look at the bloom of Siberian chrysanthemums.

A blind man is environed by the world.
The eulalia reeds on the hillside
and below them the red leaves of the lacquer trees in the valley
and the fields beyond –
these shall be my reply
as they all grow dark.
Autumn's come. I've absolutely no place to go.

A Certain Self-portrait

There is a border between words.

On the verge,
a stateless person in a fix.

Poet, words' bastard.

To You

Don't worry.
The wind is blowing; naked branches are swaying.

To You Again

Shoals of dozens of kinds of fish below.

Seagulls above.

Where I was born.

Chaktung (Fake)

I must include that word
in my dictionary.

It's dreadful!
Of whom am I the *chaktung*?
Of whom is that someone
the *chaktung*?

I will be sure to include this word of contraposition
that looks like a flock of migrant birds
flying one behind another through the night,
in my Dictionary of Primitive Language.

Isn't *chaktung* a dream of the real?
Isn't it a liberation from that loathsome real thing?

The recently coined Korean word 'chaktung' refers with contempt especially
to fakes that are imitations of the quality-brand merchandise that so many
Koreans chase after. [Tr.]

Maitreya, Future Buddha, Today

Dream:
Maitreya, due
in the far future,
5,670,000,000 years from now,
here already,
5,670,000,000 years early.

Moonlit night with Maitreya sitting in meditation.

How can you be so still?
Your stillness looks like flowers falling.
Come, storms,
uproot all this stillness.

Your meditation is way too bewitching.
How can you be so stunning?
Come, darkness,
obscure all this breathtaking beauty.

Today, 5,670,000,000 years later,
my life is a sea surging.

Maitreya is the name given to the Future Buddha, whose coming in a far
distant future is referred to in the poem. A much-admired Silla-period bronze
scuplture of Maitreya sitting in meditation, Korea's National Treasure No. 83,
shows the bodhisattva sitting with one leg bent resting on the other, meditating.
It is the most frequently visited object in the National Museum of Korea in
Seoul. [Tr.]

No Title

A hungry child wept.
A sick child wept.
A child that lost its mother wept.

I wept too,
and today, seventy-three, weep still.

A Letter Not Posted

I decline to shake hands with anyone.
Amidst innumerable lives and deaths,
flowers have blossomed of and by themselves, unfailing.
So my follies slumbered among the forsythia,
whose blossoms I heard as scattered songs.
A good distance off bloomed
mute white magnolias.
Summer came.
While it grew dark with the songs of cuckoos,
there was no silent emptiness anywhere.

Winter was bound to come every year, without fail.
The chilled branches cast shadows as if visitors
in whose presence I turned circumspect.
The swaying branches of oaks romped about
and hawthorn treetops beat the air
like the sticks of hourglass-drums.
The present seems some infant between past and future;
this world knows not a moment's rest.

Looking back, I recall a decade at home before several decades away.
When asked something, I could not straightway reply.
Only the wandering,
and the songs of wanderers,
had for me an air of truth.

Flowing streams unexpectedly raised up orphan-like mountains.
When at last they reached the sea, no ship in sight,
the streams vanished of their own accord.
My solitude was my freedom.

Ah, people's paths lay in countless stories.
Though no one had struck a bell for a long time,
its ancient peal returned
and was ringing afresh.
Distant villages drew nearer and murmured.
I held back my tears.
When numerous faults of mine drifted away as glittering streams,
I yearned simply to follow in their wake as if the leaf of a reed or
          stalk of eulalia.

But transience
is all attachment in this world,
the illusion of attachment.
Even the other world is a pathetic phantom fabricated by this world.
Every kind of rise and fall,
every kind of vicissitude, every kind of story, the migrant birds still
          coming and going,
far from being transient are all constants.

My mother passed away
in her eighty-fifth summer while her son was away.
On her memorial night, no words occurred to me.
Hinting that a spirit was near,
the candle flames wavered.
The late-night ritual offerings became my own at last.
As I was alive, I was also dead.
One person performs as two.
The next morning, there was goose-shit on the roof
and before the gate lay a road
leading to many others in the world.

Over the past thirty years many winds have blown.
Flags flapped and were torn,
sometimes laundry went flying unluckily from washing-lines.
Fury was the ground, pain the blue sky.
I too could not live without wind.

And without me, wind could not be wind.
My everyday life lay at the end of the line.
Siberia in winter was my place of origin,
days of snowstorm piling up one after another.
Sometimes the snow buried the plains, tragic
for starving animals with no place left to go;
sometimes, in silence, it covered fields of barley already green.
A kite flown by children who still have their Mongolian blue spots
shook loose into the sky.

In this world, when people were fatuous,
deities went with them, murmuring.
One by one, now, those gods have left,
and the world's a mud-flat at low tide.
Yet the coming of spring is no repetition.
On spring nights, in the seas' vast darkness where a few lights floated
camellias blossomed here and there unnoticed.
Oh, the many thousands of years contained in a word!
A friend who will change my face is coming, flying
from the unknown like the cries of white gulls.

Peace 3

In the word
'Peace'
I see
bloody corpses.
In the word
'Peace'
I see scenes
of blazing shells in deepest night.
Didn't they acclaim it as fireworks on Christmas Eve?
In the word
'Peace'
I see invasions and exploitation.
In the word
'Peace'
I see oil.
In the word
'Peace'
I see American airbases in Central Asia.
We will have to look for another word,
long obsolete or
newly minted,
a word no one uses.

Perhaps, the 'Shanti' of a dead language, Sanskrit,
the 'Kita'
of Malaysia,
that quiet peace,
peace for us all.

Also, the 'PyeongHwa' of Korean language,
the morning peace that sustains those ordinary days
when fathers die ahead of their sons.

Peace 7

Three-thousand-year village.
Son's
son's
son's
son's
son's
son's, son's village.

Village with its triennial entertainment
of quarrelling over water-rights for upper and lower paddies.

Village where people drink bowls of reconciling makkeolli
in the tavern on the outskirts.

In such a village
everyone
anyone
was uncle, younger brother, aunt, sister.
Sun-cheol who got stung by a bee was an elder brother.

Nowhere else
have I experienced any peace.
I have long been a dried-up well of peace.

Ah, the peace of that day when my well will be full to the brim!

Peace 8

I survived a war.
Grass flourished on the ruins,
so nights were full of insect songs.
The next day
I didn't remember how to play a reed-pipe.

Into a bomb crater,
out of nowhere, little animals came begging.
People were not the only ones beggared.

From the chimneys in villages where people had killed and been killed,
lo and behold,
evening smoke rose, if hesitantly.
Seeing that
I stood up, after bowing low.

Does peace come after one person has killed another?
No.
It is not peace.
Peace is a nameless life,
a short poem that cannot be translated,
a dialect.

Peace is your home and my yard.

Is peace a skull's grin, a skull's two eyes?
No.

FROM

Empty Sky

(2008)

One Thousand Years

The moon that is invisible tonight will surely be present a few
    days from now.

On ebb-tide mud-flats
a baby crab, completely illiterate,
will be sweetly submerged by the rising tide,
folding back its pointed eyes.
A thousand years later, not your line
but some other's will be born unexpectedly then submerged.
The history of your species is doomed.

Home

From inside the house,
a poodle's tail came out, welcoming.
From inside the house
my heart came out, rejoicing and welcoming.

I removed my helmet,
laid down my gun,
undid my bandolier.

I took off my ox-leather boots,
removed my socks, left sock first.
My bare feet emerged, pitiful
as fresh shoots beaten down.

I looked at my wife's photo.
I began to weep.

I Write in the Empty Sky

I let my ridiculous white pages fly away.
I write with my body alone,
with my soul alone.
I write in the empty sky.

Now I abandon my letters
and shout up at the empty sky.
I rage in near frenzy
at the empty sky.

Now I bury all my junk.
I ascend into the empty sky and dance.

O, that unreachable space beyond
the empty sky!

So-called Father,
so-called Mother,
so-called ancient Great Jade Emperor,
none can assume the name of the empty sky.
Gods
that have not been abolished for millennia,
gods still hovering,
and whatever else may hang around us,
in whatever state,
none can assume that name.

Now, swept away to uninhabited plains,
I repent to the empty sky
with a sobbing so inadequate...

How far I have roamed to reach this point!
Here at last,
I write a line, bowing my head to all the ages of empty sky.
I write, well, something.

In Lhasa, Tibet

I was at an altitude of some four thousand metres.
The Zangbo River sped by, fiercely.
A hat thrown in would vanish in a flash.
Turning round,
I slowed my breathing by half.

Following the octagonal path through Lhasa's Old City,
I turned like a slow spinning wheel.
Such a crowd of beggars gathered, and so jubilant!

Among them was one old beggar,
all wrinkles
and just two yellowed teeth.
He laughed like a fool,
said only one thing –
not 'Gotta few pennies?'
or anything like that,
my goodness,
my goodness,
not that kind of dull begging,
my goodness,
my goodness,
but 'You're the highest!'

Just that one phrase.
In a word,
I was astounded, really astounded.
My poor wandering soul
was brought to a full stop,
awakened in amazement.
Yesterday, today, or tomorrow
never was there or will there be such a way of begging.
No such begging would be plausible
anywhere else, anytime.

In the place I have come to,
in the places I will go back to,
in the world of thunder and lightning four thousand metres
          below,
who'd ever pay tribute to me
with empty hands,
saying 'You're the highest'?

Humbled by such extravagant respect,
how could I respond with a few pence?
So I fumbled to give him a banknote bearing a portrait of Mao
and made my escape.
On reflexion, like him,
I am doubtless the most wretched of beggars.
Days past,
and yesterday, too,
in order to lay my hands on a single line of poetry
and also on that space
between the lines,
I never stopped sucking for milk that would not come,
like a hungry baby thrusting its lips against every breast in sight.

It's been fifty years
since I first begged anxiously
for one word,
the truest word between words,
from some valley in this world,
from some slope in the world beyond,
or from some edge of the infinite
fathomless universe.

Spirit of one word!
You're the highest!
Dare I now hope to rise
to that peak of begging?

Only,
my happiness is that I'm no thief,
and my unhappiness that I'm forever a beggar,
that's all.

You are the highest.

Aged Twenty

Oh, I want to weep again in that room thick with the smell of
       mother's milk.

In my country,
a baby is one year old
the moment it's born.

In some countries
a baby is only one year old
a year after
it's born.

In my country
a baby, while still inside the mother's body
before it's born,
begins its full life in this world.

You ask my age?
I'm twenty.
In other countries I'm still nineteen.

The day after the sun set in the Yellow Sea,
the sun rose at Chongseokjeong on the East Sea.
I'm nineteen;
in my country I'm twenty.

At this moment, in Basra, Iraq,
shells of depleted uranium are still raining down.
A two-year-old baby died
who would have become a thick-eyebrowed
twenty-year-old girl.
A one-year-old newborn boy,
who would have grown into a strapping nineteen-year-old, is dying.

I'm a twenty-year-old with a pounding heart.

A Tavern

In the Sumerian epic *Gilgamesh*, composed around 2000 BC,
a hero set out in quest of the secret of immortality,
killing a lion with his bare hands,
striking down a fabulous heavenly ox,
then pushing on to the end of dry land.

At land's end
of all things there happened to be a tavern.

Siduri, the tavern's alewife, said:
Sir, have a cup of wine.
Secret? What secret?
Drink another cup of wine, then go back home.

In reality, the ocean was rising in the haze
at land's end.

What should he do?

I Will Not Write a Seven-step Poem

Before a fearsome gangster-spirit boss who says:
'If you don't improvise a poem
while you walk seven steps,
I will cut off your head.'
I refuse to compose a poem
while walking seven paces
so say: 'Very well, here's my head...
Now, off with it,
quickly, cut it off,'
and I offer my neck.
My head will fall
and go rolling, rolling away.

After which
a certain poem will restively roam the world
like some groundless rumour,
unjustifiable.

Thoughts I Have Nowadays

I've regained my reverence for oral literature,
for transmissions spoken across ten thousand years,
a million years,
a grandmother's grandmother's tales
her grandfather's tales,
the long talkspan of all those tales.

Don't thoughtlessly press on me
the virtues of silence, etc.
Don't insist
on Mallarmé's blank page.

How could you even exist,
or your day-after-tomorrow,
if there were no tales,
no trivial twice-told tales?

In Mongolia, I learned
how tales that have passed from mouth to mouth
from ear to ear
hardly reach their end
even after nine days and nine nights.

And that's not all.

In Mongolia
the moment people sat down to drink
the moment their drinking cups were filled,
they started to sing.
A whole night was not enough for all to have a turn at singing.

The truly long days of yesterday, today, tomorrow, and beyond,
were and will be sustained by stories
upon stories,
songs upon songs,
so that when they opened the door
dawn was already breaking crimson.

The next morning, in the ger
where all were sprawled asleep,
and barely a spark remained alive
within the cooling horse-dung stove,
they were exchanging lovely after-songs
in their sleep, their dreams.

How about going there to live, dear friend?

A Task

Come along.
I have a task to perform
to relieve us of Li Po's 'cares of ten thousand generations'.

I have a task to perform.
The nearer we approach ancient times, the more international;
the further away, the more domestic.

To go back to ancient times,
and soar aloft,
not only here
but here and there as well,
now and then at one and the same time,
with you.

To cast off my thousand-generation-long regrets
with you.

Tonight,
let's get drunk to the soles of our feet, you and I.

Untitled

Everything plundered 1,500 years ago
has become a national treasure.

Things stolen 150 years ago
have undercover become family heirlooms.
Other people,
those who have been other till now
have undercover become me.

Back then,
originally, 'I' never was.

This,
the other,
that old thing,
all are me.

You're my past
I'm your future.
Life in this world is a bitter thing.
Thus far my greatest failure
is that I've not become someone else,
that I've remained no one but me
desperately, to the end.

Ah, the afterlife of that spider
spinning a web with all its might!
Only when I make it into such an afterlife
might I
for the first time
become someone else.

Perchance I'd become my love I long to meet.

A Few Words

They don't disappear after weeping.

Damn it.
Damn it.
They're not foregone
with my body throbbing, aching,
after being beaten.

Even after a meagre soup of radish tops
at the end of three days' hunger,
they're not forgotten
as I gaze out at the hill before me.

Looking back, they've not been buried even by a century of
        oppression.

A few words!
Sunset at sea,
I just can't help it before I die,
this accursed gift, stupid fluff, a few words.

Moonlit Night

This is tonight fifteen hundred years ago.

The moon on its path, bewitched
by some plaintive flute sounds,
listens attentively to the world below,
listens to its heart's content,
then moves on.

The flute ceases before a soul knows
that the moon has quite set.

No enemies anywhere.

The Whisper

Rain falls.
I sit at my desk.
The desk speaks softly:
Once I was a flower, was a leaf, was a stalk.
I was a long root beneath the ground
stretching as far as yon desert oasis

A scrap of iron on the desk speaks:
I was the uvula of a stillness howling alone on moonlit nights.

The rain stops.
I go outside.
Grass, thoroughly soaked, speaks to me:
Once I was your joy and sorrow.
I was your history and songs.

Now I speak
to desk
to iron
to earth:
Once I was you, was you, was you.
Now I am you, I am you.

The Art of Clouds

You really are industrious.
Look at the ditch water,
look at the stream,
look over there at the busy river, the Seongcheon.
You really are industrious.

Look up at those clouds
above your head.
They rise again,
rise again.
Dashing eastward,
dashing westward the next day,
then pausing a while
to gaze down at the world below,
and one day, abruptly,
going off, leaving an empty space in the blue sky.
May the rest of your life
be just like the clouds, no more, no less.
May your next life
be just like the bend of the world beneath those clouds.

To Lovers

A couple sit at the waterside
by Soyang Lake in Chuncheon.
Time has contracted to one brief moment.
Now go in.
Go in
and conceive a baby.

Have a child.
Have a child.
Have labour pains.
Have another.

Now leave.
This world is too small, the world beyond is too big.
Leave
and live numerous deaths in big lands, in a multitude of countries.

Some Advice

Poems
block the path for better poems.
Poems
block the path for subsequent poems.

Poems, poems, my blue poems!

Escape somehow from the history of poetry,
from fashions of poetry,
from a hundred years of poetic authority.

Be born trembling, wild and alone.

Where Has My Frontier Gone?

(2011)

A Song in Four Lines

When I open my eyes, flowers are blooming.
When I shut my eyes, rain is falling.

When I am alive, birds sing.
When I am dead, snow falls.

Thanks

Styrofoam!
Vinyl!
Sad beansprouts
in a vinyl bag!
Plastic!
Grandmother!
Mother!
Tolstoy!

Pulling over its head all the sunsets of my last decades...
this day's setting sun!

Someone Asked

A foreigner from the north asked.
A foreigner from the south asked.

Have you
ever become wind?
Being wind,
have you ever become a seaway,
turbulent with bulging veins,
speeding on as if chased, as if pursuing,
on relentless waves,
white sails stretched taut?

Being wind, have you
ever sustained, unrewarded,
the tough way of geese,
their wings weary and bone-gaunt
after long journeys in the night sky?

Higher still,
around 13,000 metres,
have you ever become a path,
unrewarded,
for Himalayan storks borne along on the jet-stream,
wings spread wide
over the Himalayan sky-glacier?

Oh, the penalty for flight!

Have you
ever become wind?
Being wind,
being a head wind,
have you ever caressed at sunset

the most lovely sorrow
of rice seedlings
that put down fresh roots
five or six days after planting
and for the first time sway in the wind
in some peasants' paddy fields in East Asia?

Have you ever
carried
a kite a thirteen-year-old flew last winter
from a knoll in a barley field,
high,
high,
high
up into his dreams, until invisible
even in his dreams?

Oh, the descent!

Tonight, I want to be wind in secret.
I want to be the last gentle breath of a gust
nestling in someone's house
in a village bowing low before the moon,
quietly, quietly,
as a guest at dusk, or some other.

Reminiscence

The wind blew for such a long time.

The waves broke for such a long time.

Wolves had been howling on moonlit nights for such a long time.

For such a long time

the sky was blue,

so blue and blue that it cried like an ox, like a worm.

Years Later

Two men wouldn't yield for days.

It is the wind that stirs,
the flags that stir;
they, they wouldn't yield.

A few days later a man appeared,
and at a stroke defeated the two men.

It is the heart that stirs.

Fifteen hundred years later one bored man appeared and wouldn't
        yield.

The wind,
the flags,
and the heart all stir together.

Damn it, you dumb-skulls, sheer bullshit! Let's get sloshed.

This poem refers to the debates between Seon monks of the Tang dynasty
after intense meditation. [Tr.]

117

Lamentation

Now the river
will enter my books and flow alone.
One day
nobody will read my books any more.

Now the river
will enter your memories to flow quietly.
There
it will gradually fade.

Now the winding river
will resolve in someone's photo
to something like an unfastened belt.

One day,
one day,
no one will know whether it's a river or what.

I would rather
return to my country,
however backward and undeveloped.

Now the river will flow utterly exhausted until this evening, until
         tonight.
Tomorrow
it will turn into something else.
How absurd! It will never recognise who I am.

Proclamation

Discover no more.
I repeat:
discover no more.

The time when fire was discovered, and liquor, too!
We have come
much too long a way from that.

The wind is rising.
Butterflies,
quickly, alight.

We know of some 1,400,000 deep-sea species in the Pacific Ocean,
the Indian Ocean,
and the Atlantic Ocean.

How very fortunate –
some 30,000,000 species still undiscovered!
Please, leave them as they are.

Edison,
Edison
Edison,

invent no more.

Henceforth, discovering, inventing –
let every species of progress be condemned to death
and with that
every species of truth.

In Metaphors Again

Child!

In order to express you, I have nothing but metaphors.
In order to express you
I have nothing left but my rotting metaphors.
Child who still cannot speak!
Child who still cannot speak
although you are five or six,

Good for you!

Particularity is a fact,
universality a sham forcibly composed of facts.
At times
it's obstinacy.

Tofu, made of beans,
doesn't last three days.
Eat it quickly,
eat your fill.

Don't trust your fridge too much.

Child!
Child!
The so-called modern, universal metaphors encircling you
are oh so antiquated.

Child who cannot speak!
Hurry! Scout out those unknown metaphors
that forespeak the language you will use.

Child!

Taklamakan Desert

Why I'm going to the Taklamakan Desert,
why I'm going there as in the dream of a sixteen-year-old,
why I'm going to the Taklamakan Desert: the emptiness

there.

Why I'm going to the Taklamakan Desert
in broad daylight at the age of seventy-five
leaving all nouns and verbs behind:
the cry of the immense emptiness

there.

Why I'm going to the Taklamakan Desert:
I can no longer stand
the world's greed
and mine.

There,
in the company of a thousand-year-old skull.

Sunset

For someone, this world's
where he should have never been born.

Wrong.
For someone, this world's
where he should be born
not just once,
but six times
or seven times
and live six or seven times more.

The sun is just setting.

A Blank Page

Night when no poem comes.
Night of air-raids day after day by unmanned planes.
Night of an old Pashtun man
who lost two grandsons,
a son and a daughter-in-law,
all at once
in a riverside alley in Kabul.
Night of a child in a neighbouring house
who lost his right leg and starved to death.
Night when bloody muddle is life itself.
What a luxury sorrow is, and God!
What antiquated ornaments they are!

Night when no poem takes form on my blank page.

Of Late

The Khyber Pass
between Afghanistan and Pakistan.
It's really rugged, really desolate, a thousand-year impasse.

Bang!

One gunshot, so hollow a fullness.

Still You Must Be Born Again

Still you must be born.
You must be born in this defiled land.
The wind has not yet died down.
The day of the wind's birth
is the day of your birth.
You must be born.
Being born
you must let go with your first cry in the wind.
You must live three months and ten days as sweeping wind,
as sweeping wind and rain.
Ah, in this world there are babies, the reason for the world.
Growing as lovely as babies' teeth,
you must greet dawns with abundance of tears.

Still you must dream.
In this ravaged village, at the side of a river
where old salmon are held back on their way upstream,
you must restore every dream betrayed
or stolen.
There is a dream remaining for you. Tossing and turning you
        must dream it.
And the sky:
there is still the glow of twilight. And the magnificent night sea.

Still you must live.
What a monopoly,
what an obsession
life is.
Death's hostage,
what a cowardly politics, cowardly ideology
life must be.
Discarded spinning-wheels!
Scrapped water-wheels!
Abandoned neighbours!

With your eardrums that still resound with the tiny breathings in
        a handful of soil
fall asleep, wake up.
The following morning, your eyes
surprised by sunlight,
surprised by fans of dewdrops on spiders' webs
that hold, drop by drop, the morning sunlight,
you must live that day.
You must live as your smallest self.
Yet with the sorrow of rocks
and the joy of grasses
you must sing, day after day.

Eternity, infinity, these are greed.
Are not your limits you yourself?

Still you must listen to the sound of the wind.
In this betrayed city in this night
you must listen to the sound of the wind.
One of your ears must resonate
at the sound of rain falling,
the only sound from the other world
in this world.
The ears alone are peace, a silent tribute.
Decades of language –
despite misuse, abuse, violence –
is not your language you?
You must protect the nouns,
the hometown you used to look down on
from the hilltops that since have disappeared,
abolished souls,
the verbs, adverbs, sad adjectives
that vanished during the city night,
were abolished
to become a civilisation of the past,
and at length its skeleton.

Still you must rise up.
In this land of excess,
in this land of alienation,
in this land where all you can hear is the roaring of wild beasts,
in the darkness where small animals
and the little insects in swamps hold their breaths,
in cyberspace,
in endless desire
that has been hardened,
hardened again,
hardened again and again
throughout history,
in the strata of capital,
still you must be born again
and must become the ten billionth but also the first *homo erectus*.
Oh is your life itself
not someone's death?
Is someone's life
not your death?
Give death. Give and receive life
Still, be born again,
bloom as a wild aster along the road you follow. Become a bird.

How to Fly

The rasping cries
of journeying geese
on a frost-touched night.
Look how they fly: while they fly,
some before,
some behind.

Far beyond midnight one frost-touched night,
when one of them, quite worn out,
is about to fold its wings,
fold its wings
& fall to its death,
two of the others,
    Don't!
    Don't!
hold the folded wings up
on either side,
& pursue their distant migration,
some before,
some behind.
& as they head on
the reviving goose
spreads its wings,
fresh again like a newborn,
& all together they fly far, far away
whispering between themselves
as dawn breaks after frost-touched night.

& look how, when those migrating geese
land
all together
on the empty fields of Sincheolwon or Gucheolwon,

on fields left empty from last year
& fall fast asleep,
each takes a turn, awake & ready & watchful,
standing guard over its sleeping companions.

It's too much: nine times, ten times would be too many!
Have you or I ever done the same even once or twice?

At Eunpa Reservoir

I wish I had a heart like this reservoir.
I wish I had the yearning
in a heart like this
ruffled by the wind.

You've had much trouble in the first half of your life!

I wish I had a heart like this.
I wish I had that heart
making circle after circle
as when, in childhood,
I sent stones skipping over the water,
skipping over.
The rest of your life is headed your way!

I wish I had a life like this,
nothing more.
A moon in the sky,
a moon in the water.
If there is a moon in the water,
isn't the moon in my heart?
I just wish we had a life like this,
you and I.

Monologue

The lonesome communist José Saramago once said that
joy and sorrow
go together
because they are not water and oil.
I nod.
Nod.

Then I object:

Joy knows no sorrow.
Sorrow knows no joy.

I refuse sudden enlightenment.
All the dialogues in the world, frogs' night-long choruses,
ultimately they're each a monologue.
Flowers and sudden frosts on spring flowers,
each a monologue
to the very end.

What is truly amazing
is that dialogue
has never existed in this world of greed and lust,
no, not even once.
To the end, each and every aloneness
is so hard-shelled it has no sense
of having ever been alone.

A Reply

Child,
that
isn't a flower.
That isn't a butterfly.

They are nothing but shadows.
I am
too,
& from long ago.

What should you do? What should I do?

Around Midnight

I am living.

And

I am dying.

Smartly, the night wind is rising. My diaphragm begins to ache:
    right, I'm alive.

That Longing

See that tide rising in deepest night.
What is dying,
what is being born!
See the mud-flats late in the morning
where the ebb tide has licked the flats clean.
See the tide
flowing in,
ebbing out,
still unable to stop endlessly going crazy
for the moon!
the moon!
after how many millions of years.

See, then,
how industrious are the crabs and baby crabs on the mud-flats.

When the Wind Blows

When the wind blows
everything turns into a flag.
You turn into a flag
ahead of me.
And tree roots underground turn into flags
ahead of trees aboveground.
At sunset the flying birds turn into flags.
Nearly-dry laundry,
your hair, too,
these are already flags
without the slightest dissimulation.
Beneath the ocean
what would be the freedom of the fish dancing, undulating
under the pressure of the dark, deep sea,
if not as a flag unnoticed?
When the wind blows,
the grudges deep in my heart are transformed,
come rushing out as impetuous delights.

Why,
even falling
is my soaring,
soaring's flag,
the cloud's flag.

When the wind blows,
when the wind blows,
everything outside of everything
eventually turns into a flag.

When the wind blows,
at first
it becomes
a certain death
then a certain birth.

When the wind blows,
everything turns into a flag.
The sky turns into a flag, fluttering without beginning or end.

Looking at Clouds

A better life was not in the cards.

When I was nine,
grandmother died.
When I was seventeen,
maternal grandmother died.
When I was twenty-one
left-handed grandfather, drunken, died on the edge of a paddy field.
When I was about twenty-six
maternal grandfather died.
When I was forty
father died.
When I was sixty-five
mother died.
When I was seventy-five mother-in-law died after smoking three
        cigarettes.

Now it's my turn, by an infallible grace. A cloud is looking at me.
Silent, I look beyond the clouds.

The Sound of a Waterfall

On the wall
of the Emperor's bed chamber
in the royal palace
was a magnificent fresco.
Within the fresco
was a roaring waterfall.

One night He refused to sleep with either queen or concubine.

The following morning
His Majesty was irritated.
He summoned the artist.
Frowning, He spoke:
Two nights before,
and last night too,
I was unable to get a good night's sleep.
Why?
The roaring of the fresco's waterfall, all night long,
was confoundingly noisy.
Blot out the waterfall, completely,
at once.

Immediately
the waterfall was blotted out.

The next morning His Majesty awoke from deep sleep,
stretched widely
and said to the Lord Chamberlain:
Ah, last night I had a good sleep.
There was no sound of that wretched waterfall,
so my sleeping chamber was very quiet.

Cool!

Facing Death

Sea,
when I stand before your three thousand years,

all the inside of my body
will certainly and thoroughly disappear.

I am hungry.
I am hungry.

All that is left is beyond me.

Greeting Autumn

Inescapable eternal autumn has arrived.

What shall I do? Shall I ascend to heaven?
Shall I be shot and killed on this earth?

Where Has My Frontier Gone?

It's wrong, wrong, wrong.

All of the Korean peninsula is turning into Seoul.
Oh shit, a country with a crush on glitz,
on thousands of flashy *events*.
You, and I,
all of us, ditto,
are turning into New York.
We're turning into that wretched 'hub' or dub of a hub.
I say:
We're turning into the ugliest, most shameless so-called 'centre'.

The place where once we knew sorrow.
The place that was far from anywhere.
The place we could not leave.
The place we finally left
after being held back,
held back.
The mud-flat of my heart.
That place where, at sunset, we could see clearly
the biennial bloom of quince flowers.

The place that looked the same ten years before
and ten years after.
The place where we lived together
with great-grandmother whom I never once saw,
and great-grandfather, too, whom I never saw,
both there in mother's blurred mirror-stand.
The place where children never felt that
their father's generation was ancient history..
The place where an uneducated father
plowed an ancient field at dusk.
The place where truth kept to itself within a village.

The place where you fell asleep when I fell asleep.
The place where the uncle we believed dead came back alive.
The place where the land-rent was a bone-breaking seven-parts-
        to-three.
The place where people died closing their eyes, having no
strength to keep them open.
The place where people with low noses and high cheek-bones,
enduring harsh poverty, bowed to the dead on ritual nights.
The place where long-term plans were ineffective.
The place where people would gather together on rainy days.
The place where, if one died, all mourned.
The place where Kim was an uncle to Jang,
where A and B were cousins.
The place where people like Sir Magistrate never appeared.
The place where, on huge full-moon nights,
someone sharpened a kitchen knife
and slashed it gleaming through the air.
The place where meaning bowed down before meaninglessness.
The place we have left behind.

Where has my frontier gone?

Request

How many
a branch
a branch
there still must be
on which no bird has ever perched.

Do not say I'm lonesome, lonesome.

Where could there be
a branch
a branch
that has never been shaken by the wind?

Do not say I'm
in pain,
in pain.

Evening Road

This dog barks.
That dog barks.
I sober up.
They bark with all their might.

My sobered body listens with all its might.
Whites of their eyes turned up,
they bark, white foam surging across their teeth.
Ears stiffly erect,
necks quivering,
tails upright and quivering,
they bark with their backs
and bellies.
With ribs and all inner organs they bark.

They bark as if seeing their mortal enemies.

They bark on and on
until I have hurried past with sobered steps.

As if they are the only ones in the world,
they bark.
And bark.
Then
one by one they stop.
The last one ends on a weak whimper.

Stillness.

A stillness enfolding all
my ancestors lived and felt
– that stillness barks.
It barks with all its might.
I am rooted to the spot.

FROM

Fatherland Stars

(1984)

Sunlight

I really don't know what to do.
Let me swallow my spit,
and my unhappiness, too.
An honoured visitor is coming
to my tiny cell with its north-facing window.
It's not the chief making his rounds,
but a gleam of sunlight for an instant late in the afternoon,
a gleam no bigger than a square of folded pasteboard.
I go crazy; it's first love.
I hold out the palm of my hand,
warm the toes of my shy, bared feet.
Then as I prostrate myself on the floor
and bask my gaunt, unreligious face
in that scrap of sunlight, all too fleeting it slips away.
When the visitor has receded beyond the iron bars,
the room becomes several times colder and darker.
This special cell in a military prison is a photographer's darkroom.
Without sunlight I sometimes laughed like an idiot.
One day it was a coffin.
One day it was altogether the sea.
Amazing! A few have survived here.

Being alive is itself being at sea without a single sail in sight.

FROM

Songs for Tomorrow

(1992)

Mother

A woman, walking alone,
murmurs
as though she has a companion.
A woman, reading a novel,
weeps with the weeping
of a woman abandoned in the novel.
Isn't such a woman at times also someone's mother?
How can the Lady Maya of ancient India alone
or the Virgin Mary alone
be a mother?
And a woman who has no child
yet can search through the darkness after sunset,
isn't she also a mother?

A Cenotaph

(1997)

A Dance

When a north wind comes raging,
trees,
winter trees, all dance together.
I dance with them.
Eventually
the sky is irresistible,
snowflakes dance wildly.

Even bears in caves,
even snakes underground in the hills,
wake briefly from their long sleep
and, squirming in silence,
keep time to the work of the world.

BIOGRAPHICAL NOTES

Born in 1933 in Gunsan, North Jeolla Province, Korea, **Ko Un** is Korea's foremost living writer. After immense suffering during the Korean War, he became a Buddhist monk. His first poems were published in 1958, his first collection in 1960. A few years later he returned to the world. After years of dark nihilism, he became a leading spokesman in the struggle for freedom and democracy during the 1970s and 1980s, when he was often arrested and imprisoned.

He has published more than 150 volumes of poems, essays, and fiction, including the monumental seven-volume epic Mount Paekdu and the 30-volume *Maninbo* (Ten Thousand Lives) series. In recent years, more than thirty volumes of translations of his work have been published in some twenty languages. He has been invited to talk and give readings of his work at major poetry and literary festivals all over the world. See: http://www.koun.co.kr

Born in 1942 in Cornwall, **Brother Anthony of Taizé** has lived in Korea since 1980. He is an Emeritus Professor at Sogang University, and Chair-Professor at Dankook University. He has published some thirty volumes of English translations of Korean poetry and fiction, including seven volumes of work by Ko Un. He is a naturalised Korean citizen with the name An Sonjae. For more information see http://hompi.sogang.ac.kr/anthony/

Lee Sang-Wha is a professor in the English Department of Chung Ang University, Seoul, and has published six volumes of translations of English literature including two prose works by Gary Snyder.